When the Taliban took control of the Swat Valley, one girl fought for her right to an education. On Tuesday 9 October 2012, she almost paid the ultimate price when she was shot in the head at point-blank range.

Malala Yousafzai's extraordinary journey has taken her from a remote valley in northern Pakistan to the halls of the United Nations. She has become a global symbol of peaceful protest and is the youngest ever winner of the Nobel Peace Prize.

I Am Malala will make you believe in the power of one person's voice to inspire change in the world.

Malala Yousafzai, the educational campaigner from Swat Valley, Pakistan, came to public attention by writing for BBC Urdu about life under the Taliban. Using the pen name 'Gul Makai', she often spoke about her family's fight for girls' education in her community.

In October 2012, Malala was targeted by the Taliban and shot in the head as she was returning from school on a bus. She miraculously survived and continues her campaign for education.

In recognition of her courage and advocacy, Malala was awarded the Nobel Peace Prize in 2014, becoming the youngest ever recipient at just seventeen years of age. She was also honoured with the National Peace Prize in Pakistan in 2011 and the International Children's Peace Prize in 2013, and she was shortlisted for *Time* Magazine Person of the Year.

Malala continues to champion universal access to education through the Malala Fund, a non-profit organisation investing in community-led education programmes and supporting education advocates around the world.

www.malala.org

Christina Lamb is one of the world's leading foreign correspondents. She has reported on Pakistan and Afghanistan since 1987. Educated at Oxford and Harvard, she is the author of five books and has won many awards, including Britain's Foreign Correspondent of the Year five times and the Prix Bayeux, Europe's top award for war correspondents. She works for the *Sunday Times* and lives between London and Portugal with her husband and son.

Henna decorations of calculus and chemical formulae on Malala's hand, instead of the traditional flowers and butterflies

I Am Malala

*The Girl Who Stood Up for Education and
Was Shot by the Taliban*

Malala Yousafzai

with Christina Lamb

A W&N PAPERBACK

An abridged version of *I Am Malala* published in association with
Quick Reads

I Am Malala first published in Great Britain in 2013
by Weidenfeld & Nicolson

This abridged edition first published in 2016
by Weidenfeld & Nicolson
An imprint of the Orion Publishing Group Ltd
Carmelite House, 50 Victoria Embankment
London EC4Y 0DZ
An Hachette UK Company

1 3 5 7 9 10 8 6 4 2

ISBN 978 1 474 60048 4

Typeset by Input Data Services Ltd, Bridgwater, Somerset

Printed and bound by Group (UK) Ltd, Croydon, CR0 4Y

The Orion policy is to use papers that are natural, renewable and recyclable products and made from wood
in sustainable forests. The logging and manufacturing processes are
expected to conform to the environmental regulations of the country
of origin.

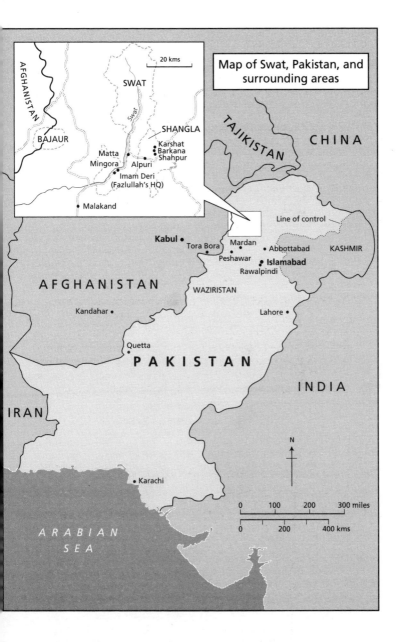

Map of Swat, Pakistan, and surrounding areas

20 kms

AFGHANISTAN

SWAT

Swat

SHANGLA

BAJAUR

Karshat
Barkana
Shahpur

Matta

Mingora
Alpuri

Imam Deri
(Fazlullah's HQ)

Malakand

TAJIKISTAN

CHINA

Line of control

Kabul

Tora Bora

Mardan

Abbottabad

KASHMIR

Peshawar

Islamabad

Rawalpindi

AFGHANISTAN

WAZIRISTAN

Kandahar

Lahore

PAKISTAN

Quetta

INDIA

IRAN

N

Karachi

0   100   200   300 miles

0   200   400 kms

ARABIAN
SEA

To all the girls who have faced
injustice and been silenced.
Together we will be heard.

Preface

My family has been through many changes. We were plucked from our mountain valley in Swat, Pakistan, and transported to a brick house in Birmingham. Sometimes it seems so strange that I want to pinch myself. I'm 17 now and one thing that has not changed is that I still don't like getting up in the morning.

My brothers and I all rush off to our different schools. And so does our mother, Toor Pekai, who is attending a language centre five days a week to learn how to read and write, and also to speak English. My mother had no education and perhaps that was the reason that she always encouraged us to go to school. She faces so many problems in her daily life, because up until now she's had difficulty communicating when she's gone shopping, or to the doctor, or the bank. Getting an education is helping her to become more confident, so that she can speak up outside the home, not just inside it with us.

Birmingham has started to feel like home. The school system here is very different from the one we had in Pakistan. In Pakistan we didn't have good science labs, computers or libraries. All we had was a teacher with a blackboard standing in front of the students and their books. I'm very busy with school and events, but I have made friends and we chat in our breaks and lunchtime.

Thanks to the extraordinary doctors here, my health is good. My hearing is better and I don't get headaches any more. I do sports, though people still take care not to throw a ball near my head!

My father, Ziauddin, is education attaché for the Pakistan consulate and an adviser for global education for the United Nations. It would be a dream life for many young, ambitious Pakistanis. But when you are exiled from your homeland, it's very painful. I see this so clearly with my mother. Physically she's in Birmingham, but mentally she's in Swat – her homesickness is horrible. All of us have been overwhelmed by the warm welcome we have received around the world and the reaction to the book, which has helped people understand our story.

With the Malala Fund, I have been to Kenya

to build a school and to Nigeria to show soli-
darity with the schoolgirls abducted by Boko
Haram militants. I have met politicians around
the globe. I've started a campaign for the education of Syrian refugees in Jordan. I have
spoken to world leaders and encouraged them
to spend more on education in their countries,
and pushed powerful nations to give more
education aid to developing countries. We are
growing our work every day, but I know there is
so much left to do. I thank God that I have been
given this platform for my campaign. This is
now my life's work, my mission and my dream.

Birmingham
July 2014

Prologue

The Day My World Changed

The day when everything changed was Tuesday, 9 October 2012. It was the middle of school exams, though as a bookish girl I didn't mind them as much as some of my classmates did.

I had started taking the school bus because my mother was scared of me walking on my own. We had been getting threats all year. After school, when our bus was called, we ran down the steps. The other girls all covered their heads before emerging from the door and climbing up into the back. It was cramped with twenty girls and three teachers. I was sitting between my best friend, Moniba, and a girl from the year below called Shazia Ramzan, holding our exam folders to our chests and our school bags under our feet.

After that it is all a bit hazy. I remember that the bus turned right off the main road at the army checkpoint, as always, and rounded the corner past the deserted cricket ground. I don't remember any more.

In reality what happened was we suddenly stopped. We couldn't see in front, but a young man had stepped into the road and waved the van down.

'Is this the Khushal School bus?' he asked our driver. The driver thought this was a stupid question as the name was painted on the side. 'Yes,' he said.

As he was speaking another young man in white approached the back of the van.

'Who is Malala?' he demanded.

No one said anything, but several of the girls looked at me. I was the only girl with my face not covered.

That's when he lifted up a black pistol. Some of the girls screamed. Moniba tells me I squeezed her hand.

My friends say he fired three shots. The first went through my left eye socket and out under my left shoulder. I slumped forward onto Moniba, blood coming from my left ear, so the other two bullets hit the girls next to me. One bullet went into Shazia's left hand. The third went through her left shoulder and into the upper right arm of Kainat Riaz.

Who is Malala? I am Malala and this is my story.

Part One

Before the Taliban

1

A Daughter Is Born

For most Pashtuns – my family's ethnic group – it's a gloomy day when a daughter is born. I was a girl in a land where rifles are fired in celebration of a son, while daughters are hidden away, their role in life simply to prepare food and give birth to children.

My father didn't care. He says he looked into my eyes after I was born and fell in love. He told people, 'I know there is something different about this child.' He even asked friends to throw dried fruits, sweets and coins into my cradle, something we usually only do for boys.

I was named after Malalai of Maiwand, the greatest heroine of Afghanistan. She inspired the Afghan army to defeat the British in 1880 in one of the biggest battles of the Second Anglo-Afghan War.

We lived in the most beautiful place in all the world. My valley, the Swat Valley, is a heavenly kingdom of mountains, gushing waterfalls and crystal-clear lakes. We have fields of wild flowers, orchards of delicious fruit, emerald mines and rivers full of trout. Even the Queen of England came, and stayed in the White Palace that was built from the same marble as the Taj Mahal by our king, the first Wali of Swat.

We lived in Mingora, the only city. Our house was one storey and made of proper concrete. On the left were steps up to a flat roof big enough for us children to play cricket on. It was our playground. At dusk my father and his friends often gathered to sit and drink tea there. Sometimes I sat on the roof too, watching the smoke rise from the cooking fires all around and listening to the crickets.

When I was born we were very poor. My father and a friend had founded their first school and we lived in a shabby shack of two rooms opposite the school. We had no bathroom or kitchen, and my mother cooked on a wood fire on the ground and washed our clothes at a tap in the school. Our home was always full of people visiting from the village. Hospitality is an important part of Pashtun culture.

Two years after I was born my brother Khushal arrived. Then, nearly five years later, another boy was born, Atal.

My mother is very beautiful and my father

adored her. Her name, Toor Pekai, means 'raven tresses', even though her hair is chestnut brown. I wished I had her lily-white skin, fine features and green eyes, but instead I inherited the sallow skin, wide nose and brown eyes of my father.

When I was around four years old I asked my father, '*Aba*, what colour are you?' He replied, 'I don't know, a bit white, a bit black.'

'It's like when one mixes milk with tea,' I said.

He laughed a lot, but as a boy he had been so self-conscious about being dark-skinned that he used to go to the fields to get buffalo milk to spread on his face, thinking it would make him lighter. It was only when he met my mother that he became comfortable in his own skin. Being loved by such a beautiful girl gave him confidence.

In our society marriages are usually arranged by families, but theirs was a love match. They came from neighbouring villages and my mother's aunt was married to my father's uncle. They glimpsed enough of each other to know they liked one another, but for us it is forbidden to express such things. Instead he sent her poems that she could not read.

'I admired his mind,' she says.

'And me, her beauty,' he laughs.

Although my mother cannot read or write, my father shares everything with her, telling her about his day, the good and the bad. She teases him a lot and gives him advice, and my father says she is always right. Most Pashtun men never do this, as sharing problems with women is seen as weak. 'He even asks his wife!' they say as an insult. I see my parents happy and laughing a lot.

My mother is very pious and prays five times a day, though not in the mosque as that is only for the men.

Growing up, we children spent most of our time with our mother. My father was out a lot as he was busy with his school, with literary societies and *jirgas* (local courts), as well as trying to save the environment, trying to save our valley. My father came from a backward village, yet through education and force of personality he made a good living for us and a name for himself.

Near us on our street there was a family with a girl my age and two boys similar in age to my brothers. We all played cricket on the street or rooftops together, but I knew as we got older the girls would be expected to stay inside and cook and serve our brothers and fathers. While boys and men could roam freely about town, my mother and I could not go out without a male relative to accompany us, even if it was a five-year-old boy! This was the tradition.

I had decided very early I would not be like that. My father always said, 'Malala will be free as a bird.' But as I watched my brothers running across the roof, flying their kites, I wondered how free a daughter could ever be.

2

My Father the Falcon

I always knew my father had trouble with words. A stutter was a terrible thing for a man who so loved words and poetry. But it was almost certainly made worse by his father, whose own voice was a soaring instrument that could make words thunder and dance.

'Spit it out, son!' he'd roar whenever my father got stuck in the middle of a sentence.

My grandfather was famous for his speeches. He taught religious studies in the government high school in the village of Shahpur. He was also an imam – a leader – at the local mosque. He was a mesmerising speaker. His sermons at Friday prayers were so popular that people would come down from the mountains by donkey or on foot to hear him.

My grandfather, *Baba*, sent my father to the government high school to learn English and receive a modern education, rather than to a madrasa (a religious school), even though as an imam people criticised him for this. *Baba* also gave my father a deep love of learning and knowledge, as well as a keen awareness of people's rights, which my father has passed on to me. In my grandfather's Friday addresses he would talk about the landowners, and how true Islam opposes the feudal system, where there is a big gap between the rich and the poor. He also spoke Persian and Arabic and cared deeply for words.

My father longed to be eloquent, with a voice that boomed out with no stammer. So when my father was thirteen he decided he would make his father proud by entering the district's annual public speaking competition. My grandfather was stunned. 'How can you?' he asked, laughing. 'You take one or two minutes to utter just one sentence.'

'Don't worry,' replied my father. 'You write the speech and I will learn it.'

Everyone thought he was mad. But eventually *Baba* gave him a fine speech, which my father practised and practised. He committed every word to memory.

When the day arrived there was a huge gathering. Other boys, some known as good speakers, gave their speeches. Finally my father was called forward. He tried desperately not to

15

think about the difficult words lying ahead of him, just waiting to trip him up and stick in his throat. When he spoke, the words came out fluently, like beautiful butterflies taking flight. His voice did not boom like his father's, but his passion shone through and as he went on he gained confidence.

At the end of the speech there were cheers and applause. As he went up to collect the cup for first prize, he saw his father clapping. 'It was,' he says, 'the first thing I'd done that made him smile.'

After that, my father entered every competition in the district. My grandfather wrote his speeches and he almost always came first, gaining a reputation locally as an impressive speaker. My father had turned his weakness into strength. For the first time *Baba* started praising him in front of others. He'd boast, 'Ziauddin is a *shaheen*' – a falcon – because this is a creature that flies high above other birds.

3

Growing Up in a School

For as long as my father could remember, it had been his dream to open a school. He thought there was nothing more important than knowledge. His own village school had been just a small building. Many of his classes were taught under a tree on the bare ground. There were no toilets and the pupils went to the fields to answer the call of nature.

Yet he says he was actually lucky. His sisters – my aunts – did not go to school at all, just like millions of girls in my country. Education had been a great gift for him. He believed that lack of education was the root of all Pakistan's problems. Ignorance allowed politicians to fool people and bad administrators to be re-elected. He believed schooling should be available for all, rich and poor, boys and girls.

When my father was offered a place for his A-levels at Jehanzeb College, which is the best college in Swat, my grandfather refused to pay for his living expenses. My father wept with frustration. If he didn't go to college, he would never be able to move out of the village and realise his dream.

My uncle taught in a local school. After my father had graduated from school he had nothing to do so he volunteered to help his brother. There his luck changed. One of my aunts had married a man in that village and they had a relative visiting called Nasir Pacha, who saw my father at work. My father told him he had just finished school and had won a college place at Jehanzeb.

'Why don't you come and live with us?' asked Nasir Pacha.

Pacha, his wife and their two sons became his second family. Their home was in Spal Bandi, a beautiful mountain village on the way to the White Palace. It was there that my father met his mentor, Akbar Khan, who although he had not gone to college himself lent my father money so he could. There my father quickly got involved in student politics and became known as a talented speaker and debater.

For the first few years after graduating from Jehanzeb my father worked as an English teacher in a well-known private college. One of my father's colleagues at the school was his dear friend Mohammad Naeem Khan. They were both frustrated as the school was very strict and unimaginative. My father longed for the freedom that would come with running his own school. So he and Naeem decided to start their own school – an English-language school in Mingora. They found the ground floor of a two-storey building in a well-off area called Landikas, with a walled courtyard where students could gather.

Naeem and my father invested their entire savings of 60,000 rupees. They borrowed 30,000 rupees more to repaint the building. They rented a shack across the road to live in, and went from door to door trying to find students. Sadly the demand for English tuition turned out to be low. It was also becoming clear that, while they were best friends, Naeem and my father found it hard to work as business partners.

Luckily another old college friend called Hidayatullah stepped in and agreed to put up the money and take Naeem's place. The new partners again went from door to door, telling people they had started a new kind of school, named the Khushal School.

However, not many people were convinced. When the school opened they had just three students.

There was worse in store when my father went to register the school and the official angled for a bribe. He joined an organisation called the Swat Association of Private Schools. The other principals took paying bribes for granted, but my father argued that if all the schools joined together they could resist. He soon became president of the Association and expanded it until it included 400 principals. Suddenly the school owners were in a position of power. Khushal School, however, was still doing so badly that they ran out of credit with the local shopkeeper and could not even buy tea or sugar.

One day my father told Hidayatullah he was going back to his village for a few days. He was actually getting married, but he didn't tell any of his friends in Mingora as he could not afford to entertain them.

Hidayatullah was horrified when my father returned to Mingora with a wife. 'We're not in a position to support a family,' he told my father.

'It's OK,' replied my father. 'She will cook and wash for us.'

Within a few months my mother was expecting a baby. Their first child, born in 1995, was a girl and stillborn.

The school continued to lose money. Months would pass and they could not pay the teachers' wages or the school rent. Just when it seemed matters could not get worse, the area was hit by flash floods. When the waters receded, they found their home and school destroyed.

It started to feel as though the school was not meant to be, but my father would not give up on his dream so easily. Besides, he had a family to provide for. I was born on 12 July 1997. My mother was helped by a neighbour who had delivered babies before.

'Malala was a lucky girl,' says Hidayatullah. 'When she was born our luck changed.'

A few months after I was born the three rooms above the school became vacant and we all moved in. The walls were concrete and there was running water. The school had five or six teachers and around a hundred pupils paying a hundred rupees a month. My father was teacher, accountant and principal. He also swept the floors, whitewashed the walls and cleaned the bathrooms. After paying the rent and salaries, there was little money left for food. We drank green tea as we could not afford milk for regular tea. But after a while the school started to break even.

Eventually Hidayatullah left to start his own school and they divided the students, each taking two of the four years. But Hidayatullah missed me so much he used to visit me. It was while he was visiting one afternoon in September 2001 that there was a great commotion. There had been a big attack on a building in New York. Two planes had flown into it. We did not realise then that 9/11 would change our world too, and would bring war into our valley.

4

The *Mufti* and the Earthquake

Just in front of the school on Khushal Street,
where I was born, was the house of a tall, hand-
some mullah and his family. His name was
Ghulamullah and he called himself a *mufti*,
which meant he was an Islamic scholar and an
authority on Islamic law. He watched the girls
going in and out of our school every day and
became angry, particularly as some of the girls
were teenagers.

One night the *mufti* gathered some of the
influential people and elders of our neighbourhood and turned up at our door. There were
seven people and they filled our small house.

'I am representing good Muslims and we all
think your girls' school is *haram* and an offence
against God. You should close it. Girls should
not be going to school,' the *mufti* said. 'There
are men in the reception area of the school, and
they see the girls enter, and this is very bad.'

'I have a solution,' said my father. 'The school

has another gate. The girls will enter through that.'

The *mufti* clearly wasn't happy as he wanted the school closed altogether. But the elders were happy with this compromise and they left.

In 2002 the President of Pakistan, General Musharraf, held elections for 'controlled democracy'. In our province these elections brought what we called a 'mullah government' to power. The Muttahida Majlis-e-Amal (MMA) alliance was a group of five religious parties which ran the madrasas (colleges) where the Taliban were trained.

The MMA government banned CD and DVD shops and wanted to create a morality police like the Afghan Taliban had set up. They launched attacks on cinemas and tore down billboards with pictures of women on them or blacked them out with paint. They even snatched female mannequins from clothing shops. They harassed men wearing Western-style shirts and trousers and insisted women cover their heads.

In 2004 General Musharraf sent the army along the border with Afghanistan. The Americans claimed that al-Qaeda militants who had fled from Afghanistan during the US bombing were using the area as a safe haven, taking advantage of our Pashtun hospitality. From

24

there they were running training camps and launching raids across the border on NATO troops.

The army retreated after just twelve days and reached what they called a 'negotiated peace settlement' with local militant leaders like Nek Mohammad. This involved the army bribing them to halt all attacks and keep out foreign fighters. The militants simply used the cash to buy more weapons and resumed their activities. A few months later came the first attack on Pakistan by a US drone – a type of military aircraft without a pilot.

On 17 June 2004 a drone attacked Nek Mohammad while he was giving an interview by satellite phone. He and the men around him were killed instantly. Then there were more attacks. The Americans said that Osama bin Laden's deputy, Ayman al-Zawahiri, was hiding in Bajaur. In January 2006 a drone supposedly targeting him destroyed three houses and killed eighteen people.

In October, another US drone hit a madrasa on a hill near the main town of Khar, killing eighty-two people, many of them young boys. The Americans said it was an al-Qaeda training camp. Within a few hours of the attack an influential local cleric announced that the deaths would be avenged by suicide bombings against Pakistani soldiers.

My father and his friends were worried and called together local elders and leaders for a peace conference. But no one would listen. Some people even laughed.

My father came home frustrated. 'I have a school, but I am neither a khan (an official) nor a political leader. I have no platform,' he said. 'I am only one small man.'

The earthquake of 8 October 2005 turned out to be one of the worst in history. It was 7.6 on the Richter scale and was felt as far away as Kabul and Delhi. Our town of Mingora was largely spared – just a few buildings collapsed – but neighbouring Kashmir and the northern areas of Pakistan were devastated. Even in Islamabad buildings collapsed.

More than 73,000 people were killed and 128,000 injured, many of them permanently disabled. Around three and a half million people lost their homes. Roads, bridges, water and power were all gone. Many of those killed were children who, like me, had been at school that morning. Some 6,400 schools were turned to rubble and 18,000 children lost their lives.

11,000 children were orphaned. In our culture

orphans are usually taken in by the extended family, but the earthquake was so bad that entire families had been wiped out or had lost everything and so were in no position to take in children. The government promised they would all be looked after by the state. But my father heard that many of the boys were housed in madrasas – a kind of welfare system as they give free food and lodging, but their teaching does not follow a normal curriculum. The boys learn the Quran by heart, rocking back and forth as they recite. They learn that there is no such thing as science or literature, that dinosaurs never existed and that men never went to the moon.

The whole nation was in shock for a long time after the earthquake. We were already so unlucky with our politicians and military dictators, and now, on top of everything else, we had to deal with a natural disaster. Mullahs preached that the earthquake was a warning from God. They said it was caused by women's freedom and obscenity. If we did not mend our ways and introduce sharia or Islamic law, they shouted in their thundering voices, more severe punishment would come.

Part Two

The Valley of Death

5

Radio Mullah

I was ten when the Taliban came to our valley. They appeared in groups, armed with knives and Kalashnikov rifles. These were strange-looking men, with long straggly hair and beards and camouflage vests over their shalwar kamiz (long shirts and baggy trousers), which they wore with the trousers well above the ankle.

Their leader was Maulana Fazlullah, a 28-year-old who had studied in the madrasa of a man called Maulana Sufi Mohammad, who had founded the militant group TNSM. Maulana Fazullah had married his daughter. When Sufi Mohammad was imprisoned in 2002, Fazlullah took over the movement's leadership.

Shortly before the earthquake, Fazlullah set up his illegal radio station. It became known as Mullah FM, and Fazlullah as the Radio Mullah.

In the beginning Fazlullah said he was an Islamic reformer and an interpreter of the Quran. He warned people to stop sinful acts like listening to music, watching movies and dancing, which had caused the earthquake. Fazlullah thundered that if people didn't stop they would again invite the wrath of God.

My father said some people liked Fazlullah's talk of bringing back Islamic law as everyone was frustrated with the Pakistani justice system.

Within six months people were getting rid of their TVs, DVDs and CDs. Fazlullah's men collected them into huge heaps on the streets and set them on fire, creating clouds of thick black smoke that reached high into the sky.

Fazlullah's broadcasts were often aimed at women. He'd say, 'Women are meant to fulfil their responsibilities in the home. Only in emergencies can they go outside, but then they must wear the veil.'

Lots of women were so moved by what Fazlullah said that they gave him gold and money. Some gave their life savings, believing that this would make God happy. Fazlullah began building a vast red-brick headquarters in Imam Deri. Every village had to take turns sending their men for a day to help build it.

One day Sufi Mohammad proclaimed from jail that there should be no education for women. My friends and I couldn't understand why it was so wrong. 'Why don't they want girls to go to school?' I asked my father.

'They are scared of the pen,' he replied.

Every day, it seemed, a new rule came. Fazlullah closed beauty parlours and banned shaving so there was no work for barbers. My father, who only has a moustache, insisted he would not grow a beard for the Taliban. The Taliban told women not to go to the bazaar.

Next Fazlullah began holding a *shura*, a kind of local court. The punishments included public whippings, which we had never seen before. His men stopped health workers giving polio drops, saying they were an American plot to make Muslim women infertile so that the people of Swat would die out.

After Mullah FM had been on air for about a year, Fazlullah became more aggressive. His men began killing khans and political activists from secular and nationalist parties. The authorities turned a blind eye.

Then we saw a letter taped to our school gate. 'Sir, the school you are running is Western and infidel,' it said. 'You teach girls and have a uniform that is un-Islamic. Stop this or you will be in trouble and your children will weep and cry for you.' It was signed, *'Fedayeen* of Islam', meaning 'Islamic sacrificers'.

My father wrote a letter to our local news-paper. 'To the *Fedayeen* of Islam, this is not the right way to implement Islam,' he wrote. 'Please don't harm my children because the God you believe in is the same God they pray to every day. You can take my life but please don't kill my schoolchildren.' Lots of people called to congratulate him. 'You have put the first stone in standing water,' they said. 'Now we will have the courage to speak.'

6

Toffees, Tennis Balls and the Buddhas of Swat

The Taliban became the enemy of fine arts, culture and our history. The Swat Museum moved its collection away for safekeeping. The Taliban blew up the face of the Jehanabad Buddha, which was carved into a hillside just half an hour's drive from Mingora and towered twenty-three feet into the sky. They took over the Emerald Mountain with its mine and began selling the beautiful stones to buy their ugly weapons.

They took money from the people who chopped down our precious trees for timber and then demanded more money to let their trucks pass. Though we still had our television, they had switched off the cable channels. My best friend, Moniba, and I could no longer watch our favourite Bollywood shows.

One day we found our teacher, Miss Hammeda, in floods of tears. Her husband was a policeman. Fazlullah's men had stormed in and some police officers had been killed, including her husband. It was the first Taliban attack on the police in our valley. Soon they had taken over many villages.

Meanwhile, the authorities, like most people, did nothing. It was as though everyone was in a trance.

The Taliban moved right into the heart of our nation's capital city, Islamabad. They raided houses they claimed were being used as massage centres, they kidnapped women they said were prostitutes and closed down DVD shops, again making bonfires of CDs and DVDs.

In July 2007 there was a siege of the Red Mosque in Islamabad which had housed Taliban militants. They called it Operation Silence, although it was very loud. Never had there been such a battle in the heart of our capital. Around a hundred people were killed, including several soldiers and a number of children. After the Red Mosque siege the Swat Taliban changed. Fazlullah gave a radio address in which he declared war on the Pakistani government.

This was the start of real trouble. There was a wave of suicide bombings across the country. There was one ray of hope – Benazir Bhutto,

the former elected prime minister, was returning from exile. The Americans were worried
that General Musharraf was too unpopular in
Pakistan to be able to stop the Taliban. They
had helped broker a power-sharing deal where
Musharraf would be a civilian president, supported by Benazir's party. In return, Musharraf
would drop corruption charges against her and
her husband and agree to hold elections, which
everyone assumed would result in Benazir becoming prime minister. No Pakistani, including
my father, thought this deal would work as
Musharraf and Benazir hated each other.

On 18 October 2007 Benazir Bhutto stepped
onto Pakistani soil after almost nine years in
exile. When she paraded on an open-top bus
through the streets hundreds of thousands of
people flocked to see her. Just before midnight
the militants struck. Benazir's bus was blown
up in a wave of orange flame. Luckily, Benazir
survived because she had gone downstairs, but
150 people were killed. It was the biggest bomb
ever to have gone off in our country. Many of
the dead were students who had made a human
chain around the bus.

About a week later the army came to Swat,
making lots of noise with their jeeps and helicopters. We ran outside and they threw toffees

and tennis balls down to us, which we rushed to catch.

One day a man told us that there would be a curfew the next day. Then we heard on the news that Musharraf had sent 3,000 troops into our valley to confront the Taliban. The following day a suicide bomber attacked an army truck in Swat, killing seventeen soldiers and thirteen civilians. Then all that night we heard the boom of cannons and machine guns from the hills. It was hard to sleep.

School was closed and we stayed at home, trying to understand what was going on. The fighting was taking place outside Mingora though we could still hear gunfire.

On 27 December 2007 a suicide bomber blew himself up by the side of Benazir Bhutto's vehicle after she had addressed an election rally. When we learned she was dead, my heart said to me, *Why don't you go there and fight for women's rights?* We were looking forward to democracy and now people asked, 'If Benazir can die, nobody is safe.' It felt as if my country was running out of hope.

7

The Diary of Gul Makai

It was school that kept me going in those dark days. We had moved up to high school and liked to be known as the clever girls.

The army action at the end of 2007 had not got rid of the Taliban. The army had stayed in Swat and were everywhere in the town, yet Fazlullah and his men still broadcast every day on the radio. Throughout 2008 the situation was even worse than before, with bomb blasts and killings.

Our school was a haven from the horrors outside. But of course at school we were under threat too, and some of my friends dropped out. Fazlullah kept broadcasting that girls should stay at home and his men had started blowing up schools.

The first school to be blown up was Shawar Zangay, a government girls' primary school in Matta. Then many more bombings followed, almost every day. On the last day of February

2008 a suicide bomber struck at Haji Baba High School. Funeral prayers had been under way for a popular local police officer, Javid Iqbal, who had been killed by a suicide bomber. Now the Taliban had bombed the mourners. More than fifty-five people were killed. Ten members of my friend Moniba's family were there and were either killed or injured. Moniba was devastated and the whole town was in shock.

'Are you scared now?' I asked my father.

'At night our fear is strong,' he told me, 'but in the morning, in the light, we find our courage again.' And this is true for my family. We were scared, but our fear was not as strong as our courage. 'We must rid our valley of the Taliban, and then no one has to feel this fear,' he said.

At school my father organised a peace march and encouraged us to speak out against what was happening. One day I went on Geo, which is one of the biggest news channels in our country. The more interviews I gave, the stronger I felt and the more support we received. I prayed to God every night to give me strength.

By the end of 2008 around 400 schools had been destroyed by the Taliban. No one would leave their homes after sunset. And then Fazlullah's deputy, Maulana Shah Dauran, announced on the radio that all girls' schools would close from 15 January.

It was during one of those dark days that my father received a call from his friend Abdul Hai Kakar, a BBC radio correspondent based in Peshawar, about 100 miles from Mingora. He was looking for a schoolgirl to write a diary about life under the Taliban. He wanted to show the human side of the catastrophe in Swat, and when the father of another girl forbade his daughter from taking part, I asked my father, 'Why not me?' I wanted people to know what was happening.

Although we had a computer there were frequent power cuts and few places had Internet access. So Hai Kakar would call me in the evening on my mother's mobile. He used his wife's phone to protect us as he said his own phone was bugged by the intelligence services. We would speak for up to forty-five minutes in Urdu, even though we are both Pashtun, as the blog was to appear in Urdu and he wanted the voice to be as authentic as possible. Then he wrote up my words and once a week they would appear on the BBC Urdu website.

Hai Kakar told me it could be dangerous to use my real name and gave me the pseudonym Gul Makai, which means 'cornflower' and is the name of the heroine in a Pashtun folk story.

My first diary entry appeared on 3 January 2009 under the heading 'I am afraid'. 'I had a terrible dream last night filled with military helicopters and Taliban. I have had such dreams since the launch of the military operation in Swat.' I wrote about being afraid to go to school because of the Taliban ruling and looking over my shoulder all the time.

It was thrilling to see my words on the website. The diary of Gul Makai received attention further afield. Some newspapers printed extracts. The BBC even made a recording of it, using another girl's voice, and I began to see that the pen and the words that come from it can be much more powerful than machine guns, tanks or helicopters.

Some of our teachers stopped coming to school. One said he had been ordered by Mullah Fazlullah to help build his centre in Imam Deri. Another said he'd seen a beheaded corpse on the way in and could no longer risk his life to teach. Many people were scared.

By the start of January 2009 there were only ten girls in my class, where once there had been twenty-seven. I kept hoping something would happen and the schools would remain open. But finally the deadline was upon us.

Wednesday, 14 January was the day my school closed. We had a special assembly that final morning but it was hard to hear with the noise of helicopters overhead. Some of us spoke out against what was happening in our valley. The bell rang for the very last time and then our headmistress, Madam Maryam, announced it was the winter holidays. But no date was announced for the start of next term. Even so, some teachers still gave us homework. In the yard I hugged all my friends. Exams were due in March, but how could they take place?

I told the documentary makers, 'They cannot stop me. I will get my education if it's at home, school or somewhere else. This is our request to the world – to save our schools, save our Pakistan, save our Swat.'

When I got home I cried and cried. I didn't want to stop learning. I was only eleven years old but I felt as though I had lost everything.

Afterwards I went on as many radio and TV channels as possible. 'They can stop us going to school but they can't stop us learning,' I said. I sounded hopeful but in my heart I was worried.

8

A Funny Kind of Peace

The BBC reporter Hai Kakar was holding secret talks with Fazlullah and his commanders. He had got to know them in interviews and was urging them to rethink their ban on girls' education.

He told Fazlullah, 'You killed people, you destroyed schools and still there was no protest in Pakistan. But when you banned girls' education people spoke out. Even the Pakistan media, which has been so soft on you till now, is outraged.'

The pressure from the whole country worked and Fazlullah agreed to lift the ban for girls up to ten years old – Year 4. I was in Year 5 and some of us pretended we were younger than we were. We started going to school again, dressed in ordinary clothes and hiding our books under our shawls. It was risky, but it was the only ambition I had back then. We were lucky, too, that Madam Maryam was brave

44

and resisted the pressure to stop working.

'The secret school is our silent protest,' she told us.

About a week after we had returned to school, on 16 February 2009, we were woken one night by the sound of gunfire. At first we thought we were in danger. Then we heard the news. The gunfire was in celebration. A peace deal had been struck between the Taliban and the provincial government.

We were happy, but we questioned how it would work. And it was hard to believe it was all over! More than a thousand ordinary people and police had been killed. Women had been kept in purdah (out of sight of men), schools and bridges had been blown up, businesses had closed. We had suffered barbaric public courts and violent justice and had lived in a constant state of fear. And now it was all to stop.

A message came from our headmistress that exams would take place in the first week of March. It was time to get back to my books.

But to our horror things didn't change much. If anything, the Taliban became even more barbaric. They were now state-sanctioned terrorists. We were disillusioned and disappointed.

But we still believed in peace. Everyone was looking forward to a big outdoor public meeting on 20 April when Sufi Mohammad, who had recently been released from prison, would address the people of Swat. He was said to be more moderate than his son-in-law, Fazlullah.

There was a huge crowd – between 30,000 and 40,000 people – but Sufi Mohammad said nothing about education. He didn't tell the Taliban to lay down their arms. Instead he appeared to threaten the whole nation. 'Now wait, we are coming to Islamabad,' he shouted.

Rather than trying to extinguish the fires of militancy, he only added fuel to the flames.

In Washington the government of President Obama seemed to be more alarmed about Pakistan than Afghanistan because our country has more than 200 nuclear warheads and they were worried about who was going to control them. They talked about stopping their billions of dollars in aid and sending troops instead.

At the start of May our army launched Operation True Path to drive the Taliban out of Swat. We heard they were dropping hundreds of commandos from helicopters into the mountains in the north. More troops appeared in Mingora too. This time they would clear the town. They announced over megaphones that all residents should leave.

9

Leaving the Valley

Leaving the valley was harder than anything I had done before. I put all my books and note-books in my school bag, then packed another bag of clothes. There was little room as we were travelling in someone else's car.

My father had resisted leaving till the end. But then some of my parents' friends had lost a relative in gunfire. Seeing their grief made my mother determined to leave. On 5 May 2009 we became IDPs. Internally Displaced Persons. It sounded like a disease.

There were a lot of us – not just us five but also my grandmother, my cousin, his wife, Honey, and their baby. My mother said I must leave my school bag because there was so little room. I was horrified. I went and whispered Quranic verses over the books to try and protect them.

Finally everyone was ready. The streets were jam-packed. Thousands of people were leaving with just the clothes they had on their backs.

We were planning to make our way to Shangla, our family village. So far, we had driven in the opposite direction, but we had had to take the only lift we could get out of Swat.

We spent our first night at Mardan. My father then left us to go to Peshawar and alert people to what was happening. He promised to meet us later in Shangla. My mother tried very hard to persuade him to come with us, but he refused.

The next day we got a lift to Abbottabad, where my grandmother's family lived. There we met up with my cousin Khanjee, who was heading north like us. He ran a boys' hostel in Swat and was taking seven or eight boys to Kohistan by coach. He was going to Besham, from where we would need another lift to take us to Shangla.

It was nightfall by the time we reached Besham, as many roads were blocked. It was not easy to get from Besham to our village and in the end we had to walk twenty-five kilometres carrying all our things.

We stayed in my mother's village, Karshat, with my uncle and his family. I was happy to be with my cousin Sumbul and once we were settled I started going to school with her.

We heard on the radio that the army had started the battle for Mingora. They had parachuted

48

in soldiers and there had been hand-to-hand fighting in the streets. The Taliban were using hotels and government buildings as bunkers.

We continued to worry about my father. In Shangla it was hard to find a mobile phone signal. We had to climb onto a huge boulder in a field, and even then we rarely had more than one bar of reception, so we hardly ever spoke to him. But after about six weeks my father said we could travel to Peshawar, where he had been staying in one room with three friends.

It was very emotional to see him again. Then, a complete family once more, we travelled down to Islamabad, where we heard that Ambassador Richard Holbrooke, the American envoy to Pakistan and Afghanistan, was holding a meeting about the conflict. My father and I managed to get inside and I took the chance to say, 'Respected Ambassador, a request, please help us girls to get an education.'

He laughed. 'You already have lots of problems and we are doing lots for you,' he replied. 'We have pledged billions of dollars in economic aid, we are working with your government on providing electricity, gas . . . but your country faces a lot of problems.'

I did an interview with a radio station called Power 99. They liked it very much and told us they had a guesthouse in Abbottabad where we could all go. We stayed there for a week and to my joy I heard that Moniba was also in Abbottabad. We arranged to meet in a park and I brought her Pepsi and biscuits.

When our week at the guesthouse ended we went to Haripur, where one of my aunts lived. It was our fourth city in two months. I knew we were better off than those who lived in the camps, queuing for food and water for hours under the hot sun, but I missed my valley. It was there I spent my twelfth birthday. Nobody remembered. Once again I wished for peace in our valley.

Part Three

Three Girls, Three Bullets

10

The Valley of Sorrows

In July 2009 our prime minister announced that the Taliban had been cleared out. He promised that the gas supply had been restored and that the banks were reopening, and called on the people of Swat to return.

As we drew close to home we all fell silent. We were worried it might have been destroyed in the shelling. We held our breath as my father unlocked the gate. The first thing we saw was that in the three months we'd been away the garden had become a jungle.

To my joy I found my school bag still packed with my books, and I gave thanks that my prayers had been answered and that they were safe. We were lucky our house had not been broken into. Four or five of the houses on our street had been looted and TVs and gold jewellery had been taken.

My father was anxious to check on the school. I went with him. The building opposite the girls' school had been hit by a missile, but the school itself looked intact. My father's keys would not work so we found a boy who climbed over the wall and opened it from the inside. We ran up the steps anticipating the worst.

'Someone has been in here,' my father said as soon as we entered the courtyard. There were cigarette stubs and empty food wrappers all over the floor. Chairs had been upended and the space was a mess. Anti-Taliban slogans were scrawled all over the walls. Bullet casings littered the floor. The soldiers had made a hole in the wall through which you could see the city below. Maybe they had even shot at people through that hole. I felt sorry that our precious school had become a battlefield.

Fazlullah himself was still at large and I was afraid the Taliban would regroup and return to power. My father's friend Ahmad Shah called it a 'controlled peace, not a durable peace'. But gradually people returned to the valley because Swat is beautiful and we cannot bear to be away from it for long.

Our school bell rang again for the first time on 1 August. I was overjoyed to see all my old friends. We had so many stories from our time as IDPs.

That summer twenty-seven girls from the Khushal School were invited to spend a few days in Islamabad, seeing the sights and taking part in workshops to help us get over the trauma of living under the Taliban. There were six from my class and we were looked after by my mother and Madam Maryam.

Islamabad was totally different to Swat. It was as different for us as Islamabad is to New York. We met women who were lawyers and doctors and also activists, which showed us that women could do important jobs and yet still keep their culture and traditions.

We also met Major General Athar Abbas, the chief spokesman for the army and its head of public relations. All of us girls made it clear that we wanted to see the Taliban brought to justice, but we weren't very convinced this would happen. Afterwards, General Abbas gave some of us his visiting cards and told us to contact him if we ever needed anything.

We'd had a wonderful time and when we got back to Swat I felt so hopeful about the future that I planted a mango seed in the garden during the fast of Ramadan. Mangos are a favourite fruit to eat after breaking the fast.

But my father had a big problem. While we had been IDPs, and for all the months the school had been closed, he had collected no fees, but the teachers still expected to be paid. They had their own expenses and one of them, Miss Hera, was about to get married and had been relying on her salary to help pay for the ceremony.

Altogether that would be over one million rupees. Then we remembered General Abbas and his visiting card. It was because of the army operation to expel the Taliban that we had all had to leave and that we found ourselves in this situation now. So Madam Maryam and I wrote to General Abbas explaining the situation. He was very kind and sent us 1,100,000 rupees so my father could pay everyone three months' back pay. The teachers were so happy. Miss Hera called my father in tears, grateful that her wedding could go ahead as planned.

This didn't mean we went easy on the army. We were very unhappy about the army's failure to capture the Taliban leadership, and my father and I continued to give lots of interviews.

Around the time I turned thirteen, in July 2010, the rain came. It was relentless and so heavy that you couldn't even see the person standing in front of you. Environmentalists had warned that our mountains had been stripped of trees by the Taliban and timber smugglers. Soon muddy floods were raging down the valleys, sweeping away everything in their wake.

We were in school when the floods started and were sent home. It took days for the water to drain away and when we returned we could see chest-high tide marks on the walls. There was mud, mud, mud, everywhere. There was so much damage that it cost my father 90,000 rupees to repair – equivalent to the monthly fees for ninety students. Thirty-four of our forty-two bridges had been washed away, cutting off much of the valley. Electric pylons had been smashed to pieces, so we had no power.

No one could understand how this had happened. People had lived by the river in Swat for 3,000 years and always seen it as our lifeline, not a threat, and our valley as a haven from the outside world. Now we had become 'the Valley of Sorrows', said my cousin Sultan Rome. People were desperately worried that the Taliban would take advantage of the chaos and return to the valley. While all this suffering was going on our president, Asif Zardari, was on holiday at a chateau in France.

Even when the rains finally ceased life was still very difficult. We had no clean water and no electricity. In August we had our first case of cholera in Mingora and soon there was a tent of patients outside the hospital.

In Swat we began to see more signs that the Taliban had never really left. Two more schools were blown up and three foreign aid workers from a Christian group were kidnapped and murdered. We received other shocking news. My father's friend Dr Mohammad Farooq, the vice chancellor of Swat University, had been killed by two gunmen who burst into his office.

We felt frustrated and scared once again. When we were IDPs I had thought about becoming a politician and now I knew that was the right choice. Our country had so many crises and no real leaders to tackle them.

11

Praying to Be Tall

When I was thirteen I stopped growing. I had always looked older than I was but suddenly all my friends were taller than me. I was speaking at a lot of events, but because I was so short it wasn't easy to be authoritative. Sometimes I could hardly see over the lectern. I did not like high-heeled shoes but I started to wear them.

One Monday I was about to measure myself against the wall to see if I had miraculously grown in the night when I heard loud voices next door. My father's friends had arrived with news that was hard to believe. During the night American special forces called Navy Seals had carried out a raid in Abbottabad, one of the places where we'd stayed as IDPs, and had found and killed Osama bin Laden. He had been living in a large walled compound less than a mile from our military academy. We couldn't believe the army had not known where bin Laden was.

At first we assumed our government had

known and had been involved in the American operation. But we soon found out that the Americans had gone it alone. This didn't sit well with our people. My father said it was a shameful day. 'How could a notorious terrorist be hiding in Pakistan and remain undetected for so many years?' he asked. Others were asking the same thing.

In October 2011 my father told me he had received an email informing him I was one of five nominees for the international peace prize of KidsRights, a children's campaign group based in Amsterdam. My name had been put forward by Archbishop Desmond Tutu from South Africa. He was a great hero of my father's for his fight against apartheid. My father was disappointed when I didn't win, but I pointed out to him that all I had done was speak out. We didn't have an organisation doing practical things like the award winners had.

Shortly after that I was invited by the chief minister of Punjab, Shahbaz Sharif, to speak in Lahore at an education gala. He was building a network of new schools, called Daanish Schools, and giving free laptops to students. To motivate pupils in all provinces he was giving cash awards to girls and boys who scored well in their exams. I was presented with a cheque for my campaign for girls' rights.

I spoke at the gala about how we had defied the Taliban edict and carried on going to school secretly. 'I know the importance of education because my pens and books were taken from me by force,' I said. 'But the girls of Swat are not afraid of anyone. We have continued with our education.'

Then I was awarded Pakistan's first ever National Peace Prize.

The ceremony was on 20 December 2011 at the prime minister's official residence in Islamabad. After the prime minister had presented me with the award and a cheque, I presented him with a long list of demands. I told him that we wanted our schools rebuilt and a girls' university in Swat. I knew he would not take my demands seriously, so I didn't push very hard. I thought, *One day I will be a politician and do these things myself.*

It was decided that the prize should be awarded annually to children under eighteen years old and be named the Malala Prize in my honour. My father was not very happy with this. Like most Pashtuns, he is a bit superstitious. In Pakistan we don't have a culture of honouring people while they are alive, only the dead, so he thought it was a bad omen. I know my mother didn't like the awards because she feared I would become a target as I became more well-known.

I had received many awards and prizes by the end of that year and I wanted to start an education foundation. This had been on my mind ever since I had seen some children working on a rubbish mountain. I still could not shake off the image of the black rats I had seen there. And I could not forget a girl with matted hair sorting rubbish into piles, one for cans, one for bottle tops, another for glass and another for paper. She would sell these piles for a few rupees. I vowed I would do everything in my power to help educate girls just like her.

In January 2012 we went to the city of Karachi as guests of Geo TV after the government of Sindh province announced they were renaming a girls' secondary school on Mission Road in my honour. My brother Khushal was now at school in Abbottabad, so it was just me, my parents and my brother Atal.

We flew to Karachi and it was the first time any of us had ever been on a plane. I was amazed by the number of people and houses and cars. Karachi is one of the biggest cities on earth, with around twenty million people. It's actually the largest Pashtun city in the world as between five and seven million Pashtuns have gone there to work.

We went to the Sindh assembly, then we went to visit some schools, including the one that was being named after me. I made a speech about the importance of education. It was both odd and wonderful to see my name on a school.

There was one important place we had to include in our visit to Karachi besides our out-ings to the sea and the huge bazaars, where my mother bought lots of clothes. We needed to visit the tomb of Pakistan's founder and great leader, Mohammad Ali Jinnah. The peaceful building felt sacred to us.

A Pakistani journalist living in Alaska turned up at our hostel. She wanted to meet me after she had seen a documentary about us on the *New York Times* website. She chatted with me for a while, then she went on the internet and showed us that the Taliban had that day issued threats against two women – Shad Begum, an activist in Dir, and me, Malala. 'These two are spreading anti-religious messages and should be killed,' it said.

After that my father was restless and could

not enjoy Karachi. I could see my mother and father were both very upset.

'Maybe we should stop our campaigning and go into hibernation for a time,' said my father.

'How can we do that?' I replied. 'You were the one who said if we believe in something greater than our lives, then our voices will only multiply even if we are dead. We can't disown our campaign!'

People were asking me to speak at events. We couldn't refuse because of a security problem, especially not as proud Pashtuns.

Still, it was with a heavy heart that we returned to Swat. My father went to the police and they showed him a file on me. They told him that my national and international profile meant I had attracted attention and death threats from the Taliban and that I needed protection. They offered us guards, but my father was not keen. Many elders in Swat had been killed despite having bodyguards, and the Punjab governor had been killed by his own bodyguard. My father also thought armed guards would alarm the parents of the students at school, and he didn't want to put others at risk. When he had had threats before he always said, 'Let them kill me but I'll be killed alone.'

He suggested sending me to boarding school

in Abbottabad, like my brother, but I didn't want to go.

At home I started bolting the main gate of our house at night.

12

Who Is Malala?

On 12 July 2012 I turned fifteen, which in Islam means you are an adult. With my birthday came the news that the Taliban had killed the owner of the Swat Continental Hotel, who was on a peace committee. Once again people started worrying that the Taliban were creeping back.

It was late in the evening of 3 August when my father received an alarming phone call from the nephew of his friend Zahid Khan. He told us that his uncle had been shot in the face and was in hospital.

When he heard the news, my father said the earth fell away from his feet. 'It was as if I had been shot,' he said. 'I was sure it was my turn next.'

After that our phone did not stop ringing with people calling to warn my father he could be the next target, but he again refused to have a police guard. 'If you go around with a lot of security the Taliban will use Kalashnikovs or suicide bombers and more people will be killed,' he said. 'At least I'll be killed alone.' Nor would he leave Swat. 'Where can I go?' he asked my mother. 'I cannot leave the area. I am president of the Global Peace Council, the spokesperson of the council of elders, the president of the Swat Association of Private Schools, director of my school and head of my family.'

His only precaution was to change his routine. One day he would go to the primary school first, another day to the girls' school, the next day to the boys' school. I noticed that wherever he went he would look up and down the street four or five times.

Despite the risks, my father and his friends continued to be very active, holding protests and press conferences.

After the threats against me, my mother didn't like me walking anywhere and insisted I get a rickshaw to school and take the bus home, even though it was only a five-minute walk.

At night I would wait until everyone was asleep then I'd check every single door and window. I'd go outside and make sure the front gate was locked. Then I would check all the rooms, one by one. My room was at the front, with lots of windows, and I kept the curtains open. I wanted to be able to see everything, though my father told me not to.

Then I'd pray. At night I used to pray a lot. The Taliban think we are not Muslims, but we are. We believe in God more than they do and we trust him to protect us. The time of year I prayed most was during exams, though our teachers used to warn us, 'God won't give you marks if you don't work hard. God showers us with his blessings, but he is honest as well.'

So I studied hard, too. The night before the exams began I stayed up studying until three o'clock in the morning and reread an entire textbook.

The first paper, on Monday, 8 October, was physics. I love physics because it is about truth, a world determined by principles and laws – no messing around or twisting things like in politics, which happens a lot in my country. The next day was Pakistan studies, a difficult paper for me. Once again I stayed up late, learning by heart the textbook about the history of our independence.

In the morning my parents came to my room as usual and woke me up. My mother made our usual breakfast of sugary tea, chapatis and fried egg. It was a big day for my mother as that afternoon she was going to one of her first lessons to learn to read and write with Miss Ulfat, my old teacher from nursery school.

The Pakistan studies paper went better than I thought it would. I answered all the questions and was confident I'd done well. I was happy when the exam was over, chatting and gossiping with my friends as we waited for Sher Mohammad Baba, a school assistant, to call for us when the bus arrived.

At twelve o'clock Baba called us over the loudspeaker. We all ran down the steps. The other girls covered their faces before emerging from the door and climbed into the back of the bus. I wore my scarf over my head but never over my face.

Usman Bhai Jan started the bus and we were off. I was talking to Moniba, my wise, nice friend. Moniba and I liked to sit near the open back so we could see out. At that time of day Haji Baba Road was always a jumble of coloured rickshaws, people on foot and men on scooters, all zigzagging and honking. The air smelt of diesel, bread and kebab mixed with the stink from the stream where people still dumped their rubbish – and were never going to stop, despite all of the campaigning by my father and his friends.

The bus turned right off the main road at the army checkpoint.

The road up the small hill is usually busy as it is a short cut, but that day it was strangely quiet. 'Where are all the people?' I asked Moniba. All the girls were singing and chatting and our voices bounced around inside the bus.

I didn't see the two young men step out into the road and bring the van to a sudden halt. I didn't get a chance to answer their question, 'Who is Malala?' or I would have explained to them why they should let us girls go to school, as well as their own sisters and daughters.

Part Four

Between Life and Death

13

'God, I entrust her to You'

As soon as Usman Bhai Jan realised what had happened he drove to Swat Central Hospital at top speed. The other girls were screaming and crying. I was lying on Moniba's lap, bleeding from my head and left ear.

The news spread quickly. My father was at the Swat Press Club for a meeting of the Association of Private Schools. He had just gone on stage to give a speech when his mobile rang. He recognised the number as the Khushal School and passed the phone to his friend Ahmad Shah to answer. 'Your school bus has been fired on,' he whispered urgently to my father.

The colour drained from my father's face. He immediately thought, *Malala could be on that bus!*

As soon as he had finished speaking, my father rushed off to the hospital with Ahmad Shah and another friend, Malik Riaz, who had a car. They arrived to find crowds gathered outside and photographers and TV cameras. Then he knew for certain that I was there. My father's heart sank. He pushed through the people and ran through the camera flashes into the hospital. Inside, I was lying on a trolley, a bandage over my head, my eyes closed, my hair spread out.

'My daughter, you are my brave daughter, my beautiful daughter,' he said over and over, kissing my forehead and cheeks and nose. He had always believed that if the Taliban came for anyone, it would be for him, not me. He said he felt as if he had been hit by a thunderbolt. 'They wanted to kill two birds with one stone. Kill Malala and silence me for ever.'

The doctors reassured him that they had done a CT scan which showed that the bullet had not gone near my brain. They cleaned and bandaged the wound.

'O Ziauddin! What have they done?' Madam Maryam burst through the doors. She had not been at school that day but was at home nursing her baby when she received a phone call from her brother-in-law checking she was safe. Alarmed, she switched on the TV and saw the headline that there had been a shooting on the Khushal School bus. As soon as she heard I had been shot, she called her husband. He brought her to the hospital on the back of his motorbike, something very rare for a respectable Pashtun woman. 'Malala, Malala. Do you hear me?' she called.

I grunted.

Maryam saw the two other Khushal girls who had been shot. Shazia had been hit twice, in the left collarbone and palm, and had been brought to the hospital with me. Kainat had not realised she was hurt to start with and had gone home then discovered she had been grazed by a bullet at the top of her right arm, so her family had brought her in.

At 3 p.m. the local army commander arrived and announced they were sending an army helicopter to take me and my father to Peshawar. There wasn't time to fetch my mother, so Maryam insisted she would go too as I might need a woman's help.

Down below, my mother was watching from the roof of our house. When she heard that I had been hurt she was having her reading lesson with Miss Ulfat. One of my father's friends phoned her to tell her I was being taken to Peshawar by helicopter and she should come by road. Then they heard the sound of the helicopter.

The helipad was just a mile from our house and all the women rushed up to the roof. 'It must be Malala!' they said. As they watched the helicopter fly overhead, my mother took her scarf off her head, an extremely rare gesture for a Pashtun woman. She lifted her scarf up to the sky, holding it in both hands as if it was an offering. 'God, I entrust her to You,' she said to the heavens.

Inside the helicopter I was vomiting blood. My father was horrified, but then Maryam noticed me trying to wipe my mouth with my scarf. 'Look, she is responding!' she said. 'That's an excellent sign.'

When we landed in Peshawar they were alarmed to be taken to CMH, the Combined Military Hospital. CMH is a large sprawling brick hospital with 600 beds and dates from the time of British rule.

I was rushed to the intensive care unit. A young man came in and introduced himself as Colonel Junaid, a neurosurgeon. My father didn't think he looked like a doctor because he seemed so young.

Colonel Junaid examined me. I was conscious and restless but not speaking or aware of anything, my eyes fluttering. The colonel stitched the wound above my left brow where the bullet had entered, but he was surprised not to see any bullet in the scan. 'If there is an entry there has to be an exit,' he said. He located the bullet lying next to my left shoulder blade. 'She must have been stooping so her neck was bent when she was shot,' he said.

They took me for another CT scan. Then the colonel called my father into his office, where he had the scans up on a screen. He told him that the scan in Swat had been done from only one angle, but this new scan showed the injury was more serious. 'The CT scan shows the bullet went very close to the brain.' He said particles of bone had damaged the brain membrane. 'We can pray to God. Let's wait and see,' he said. 'We're not going to operate at this stage.'

Afterwards, my father found out that despite his youthful appearance Colonel Junaid had been a neurosurgeon for thirteen years. He was the most experienced and decorated neurosurgeon in the Pakistani army.

The next few hours were a wait-and-see time, the nurses monitoring my heartbeat and vital signs. Sometimes I made a low grunt and moved my hand or fluttered my eyes.

Late in the evening my mother came with Atal. They had made the four-hour journey by road, driven by a friend of my father's. Before she arrived, Maryam and my father had called her and told her to prepare for the worst.

When my mother arrived they hugged and held back tears.

Atal was overwhelmed and cried a lot. 'Mama,' he wept, 'Malala is hurt so badly.'

My mother was in a state of shock and could not understand why the doctors were not operating to remove the bullet. Atal was making so much noise that eventually an orderly took them to the hospital's military hostel, where they were to be put up.

Around midnight Colonel Junaid told my father I had started to get worse. My consciousness was fading and I had again been vomiting blood. Colonel Junaid ordered a third CT scan. This showed that my brain was swelling dangerously.

'But I thought the bullet hadn't entered her brain,' said my father.

Colonel Junaid explained that a bone had fractured and splinters had gone into my brain, creating a shock and causing it to swell. He needed to remove some of my skull to give the brain space to expand. 'We need to operate now to give her a chance,' he said.

Cutting away some of my skull sounded very

drastic to my father. It was a brave decision by Colonel Junaid. It was a decision that would save my life. My father's hand shook as he signed the consent papers. There in black and white were the words 'the patient may die'.

They started the operation around 1.30 a.m. My mother and father sat outside the operating theatre, praying.

Inside the theatre Colonel Junaid used a saw to remove an eight-to-ten-centimetre square from the upper-left part of my skull so my brain had space to swell. He then cut into the tissue on the left of my stomach and placed the piece of bone inside to preserve it until they could put it back. Then he cut a hole in my throat, an operation called a tracheotomy, as he was worried the swelling was blocking my airway. He also removed clots from my brain and the bullet from my shoulder blade. After all this I was put on a ventilator to help me breathe. The operation took almost five hours.

The next morning the news was good. I had moved my arms. Then three top surgeons from the province came to examine me. They said Colonel Junaid had done a splendid job. The operation had gone very well, but I should now be put into an induced coma because if I woke up there would be pressure on the brain.

While I was hovering between life and death, the Taliban issued a statement claiming that they were responsible for shooting me. 'Malala has been targeted because of her pioneer role in preaching anti-religious messages . . . She was young but she was promoting Western culture in Pashtun areas. She was pro-West, she was speaking against the Taliban, she was calling President Obama her idol.'

Then around 3 p.m. in the afternoon two British doctors arrived by helicopter from Rawalpindi. Dr Javid Kayani and Dr Fiona Reynolds were from hospitals in Birmingham. They happened to be in Pakistan advising the army on how to set up the country's first liver transplant programme. The army chief, General Kayani, had asked the doctors to brief him on their progress before flying home, and this happened to be the morning after I had been shot.

General Kayani and Dr Javid Kayani were not related, but they knew each other well and so the general asked the doctor to assess me before flying back to the UK. Dr Javid, who is an emergency care consultant at Queen Elizabeth Hospital in Birmingham, agreed, but asked to bring Dr Fiona as well, as she is from Birmingham Children's Hospital and a specialist in children's intensive care.

Colonel Junaid and the hospital director were not pleased to see them. There was some argument until Dr Javid made it clear who had sent them. The British doctors were not happy with what they found. Dr Fiona said I had had the right surgery at the right time, but my chances of recovery were now being compromised by the aftercare. After neurosurgery it is essential to monitor breathing and gas exchange (the exchange of oxygen and carbon dioxide), and carbon dioxide levels should be kept in the normal range. Then they left in their helicopter because it is dangerous to be in Peshawar after dark.

14

Journey into the Unknown

I was shot on a Tuesday at lunchtime. Late on Wednesday night two military doctors who were intensive care specialists had arrived from Islamabad. They had been sent by General Kayani after the British doctors had reported back to him that if I was left in Peshawar I would suffer brain damage and might even die because of the quality of the care and the high risk of infection. They wanted to move me but suggested that in the meantime a top doctor be brought in.

The hospital staff had made none of the changes Dr Fiona had recommended and my condition got worse as the night went on. Infection had set in. On Thursday morning one of the specialists called Dr Fiona. 'Malala is now very sick,' he told her. Dr Fiona was about to leave for the airport to fly back to Birmingham, but when she heard the news she offered to help and two nurses from her hospital in

Birmingham also stayed on with her.

She arrived back in Peshawar at lunchtime on Thursday. She told my father that I was to be airlifted to an army hospital in Rawalpindi, which had the best intensive care. He couldn't see how a child so sick could fly, but Dr Fiona assured him that she did this all the time, so not to worry. He asked her if there was any hope for me. 'Had there been no hope I would not be here,' she replied. My father says that in that moment he could not hold back his tears.

As soon as we landed in Rawalpindi we were taken by ambulance, with a military escort, to a hospital called the Armed Forces Institute of Cardiology. My father was alarmed – how would they know how to deal with head wounds? But Dr Fiona assured him it had the best intensive care in Pakistan, with state-of-the-art equipment and British-trained doctors. Her own nurses from Birmingham were waiting there and had told the cardiology nurses in great detail how to deal with head injuries. They spent the next three hours with me, swapping my antibiotics and my blood lines as I seemed to be reacting badly to the blood transfusions. Finally they said I was stable.

The hospital had been put on complete lock-down. The security seemed astonishing, but over the last three years the Taliban had managed to get into and attack even the most highly guarded military installations.

Dr Fiona was a great comfort to us. My mother speaks only Pashto, so she couldn't understand anything she said, but Fiona would gesture with a thumbs-up when she came out of my room and say, 'Good.' She became a messenger for my parents, not just a doctor. She would sit with them patiently and would then ask my father to explain every detail to my mother. My father was astonished and pleased – in our country few doctors bother explaining anything to a woman who can't read or write.

My parents heard that offers were pouring in from overseas to treat me, including from America where a top hospital called Johns Hopkins had offered free treatment. There were offers, too, from Germany, Singapore, the United Arab Emirates and Britain.

General Kayani asked whether I should be sent abroad or not. Perhaps more than any politician he understood the political implications if I did not survive. Dr Fiona said it was likely I would have a speech impediment and a weak right arm and right leg, so I would need extensive rehabilitation facilities, which Pakistan did not have. 'If you're serious about getting the

84

best outcome possible, take her overseas,' she advised.

Queen Elizabeth Hospital in Birmingham is known for treating British soldiers wounded in Afghanistan and Iraq. Its location outside the centre of the city also offered privacy. Dr Javid called his boss, Kevin Bolger, the hospital's chief operating officer. He quickly agreed it was the right thing to do, although it was not a simple exercise. Bolger soon found himself tangled in the hoops of British and Pakistani red tape. Meanwhile time was ticking away.

Finally the go-ahead was given and the doctors had the problem of how I was to be moved and who would pay for it. Dr Javid suggested taking up an offer from the Royal Air Force as they were used to transporting wounded soldiers from Afghanistan, but General Kayani refused. Luckily the ruling family of the United Arab Emirates stepped in and offered their private jet, which had its own on-board hospital. I was to be flown out of Pakistan for the first time in my life in the early hours of Monday, 15 October.

On Sunday afternoon my father was informed by the colonel that I would be leaving the next morning for the UK and only he was to accompany me.

85

But my father said, 'I can't leave my wife and sons alone here. They are at risk.' We were all at risk from a Taliban attack. My father had been told that even my brothers would not be spared.

This caused a big problem, because I was a child so I couldn't be sent alone. My father then signed a document making Dr Fiona my guardian for the trip to the UK. He was in tears as he gave her my passport and took her hand. 'Fiona, I trust you. Please take care of my daughter.'

Then my mother and father came to my bedside to say goodbye. My mother cried, but my father tried to comfort her as he felt I was now out of danger. My family trusted that Dr Fiona and Dr Javid would give me the best possible care.

I was taken away at 5 a.m. on Monday, 15 October, under armed escort. I am told the United Arab Emirates plane is the height of luxury, with a plush double bed, sixteen first-class seats and a mini-hospital at the back staffed with European nurses led by a German doctor. I am just sorry I wasn't conscious to enjoy it. The plane flew to Abu Dhabi for refuelling then headed on to Birmingham, where it landed in the late afternoon.

In the hostel my parents waited. They assumed their passports and visas were being processed and they would join me in a few days. But they heard nothing. They had no phone and no computer to check on my progress. The wait felt endless.

Part Five

A Second Life

15

'The Girl Shot in the Head, Birmingham'

I woke up on 16 October, a week after the shooting. I was thousands of miles away from home, with a tube in my neck to help me breathe and unable to speak. The first thing I thought when I came round was, *Thank God I'm not dead*. But I had no idea where I was. The nurses and doctors were speaking English, though they seemed all to be from different countries. I was speaking to them, but no one could hear me because of the tube in my neck. To start with my left eye was very blurry and everyone had two noses and four eyes. *Where was I? Who had brought me here? Where were my parents? Was my father alive?* I was terrified.

Dr Javid, who was there when I was brought round, says he will never forget the look of fear and bewilderment on my face. He spoke to me in Urdu. A nice lady in a headscarf held my hand and said, '*Assalamu alaikum*,' which is our traditional Muslim greeting. Then she started saying prayers in Urdu and reciting verses of the Quran. She told me her name was Rehanna and she was the Muslim chaplain. Her voice was soft and her words were soothing, and I drifted back to sleep.

When I woke again the next day I noticed I was in a strange green room with no windows and very bright lights. It was an intensive care cubicle in the Queen Elizabeth Hospital. Everything was very clean and shiny, not like the hospital in Mingora.

A nurse gave me a pencil and a pad, but I couldn't write properly. Dr Javid brought me an alphabet board so I could point to the letters. The first words I spelled out were 'father' and 'country'. The nurse told me I was in Birmingham, but I had no idea where that was.

My head was aching so much that even the injections they gave me couldn't stop the pain. My left ear kept bleeding and my left hand felt funny. Nurses and doctors kept coming in and out. The nurses asked me questions and told me to blink twice for yes. No one told me what was going on or who had brought me to the hospital. I could feel that the left side of my face wasn't working properly. If I looked at the nurses or doctors for too long my left eye watered. I didn't seem to be able to hear from my left ear and my jaw wouldn't move properly. I gestured to people to stand on my right.

Later, Dr Fiona came and gave me a white teddy bear. She said I should call it Junaid and she would explain why later. I didn't know who Junaid was, so I named it Lily. She also brought me a pink exercise book to write in. The first two questions my pen wrote were, 'Why have I no father?' and 'My father has no money. Who will pay for all this?'

'Your father is safe,' she replied. 'He is in Pakistan. Don't worry about payment.'

Those first days, my mind kept drifting in and out of a dream world. I thought I had been shot but wasn't sure – were these dreams or memories? I was obsessed by how much this must be costing.

The only thing that calmed me was when Rehanna came. She said healing prayers and I started moving my lips to some of them and mouthing 'Amin' (our word for 'amen') at the end. The television was kept off, except once when they let me watch *Masterchef* which I used to watch in Mingora and loved, but everything was blurred. It was only later I learned that people were not allowed to bring in newspapers or tell me anything, as the doctors were worried it could traumatise me.

I was terrified that my father could be dead. Then Fiona brought in a Pakistani newspaper from the week before. It had a photograph of my father talking to General Kayani, with a shawled figure sitting at the back next to my brother. I could just see her feet. 'That's my mother!' I wrote.

Later that day Dr Javid came in with his mobile phone. 'We're going to call your parents,' he said. My eyes shone with excitement. He dialled the number, spoke and then gave me the phone.

There was my father's voice. I couldn't talk because of the tube in my neck. But I was so happy to hear him. I couldn't smile because of my face, but there was a smile inside. 'I'll come soon,' he promised. The call did not last long because my parents did not want to tire me out. My mother blessed me with prayers.

'Mirror,' I wrote in the pink diary. The nurses brought me a small white mirror that I still have. When I saw myself, I was distraught. My long hair had gone, and the left side of my head had none at all – the Pakistani doctors had shaved my head. My face was distorted as if someone had pulled it down on one side, and there was a scar to the side of my left eye.

'Who did this to me?' I wrote, my letters scrambled. 'What happened to me?'

'Something bad happened to you,' said Dr Fiona.

She told me that I had been shot on the school bus. She said two of my friends on the bus had also been shot, but I didn't recognise their names. She explained that the bullet had entered through the side of my left eye where there was a scar, travelled eighteen inches down to my left shoulder and stopped there. It could have taken out my eye or gone into my brain. It was a miracle I was alive.

On the fifth day I got my voice back and I talked to my parents on Dr Javid's phone. I was worried about sounding strange. 'Do I sound different?' I asked my father.

'No,' he said. 'You sound the same and your voice will only get better. Are you OK?' he asked.

'Yes,' I replied, 'but this headache is so severe, I can't bear the pain.'

My father got really worried. I think he ended up with a bigger headache than me. In all the calls after that he would ask, 'Is the headache increasing or decreasing?'

After that I just said to him, 'I'm OK.' I didn't want to upset him and didn't complain even when they took the staples from my head and gave me big injections in my neck. 'When are you coming?' I kept asking.

By then they had been stuck in the army hostel at the hospital in Rawalpindi for a week with no news about when they might come to Birmingham. My mother was so desperate that she told my father, 'If there is no news by tomorrow I will go on a hunger strike.' Later that day my father went to see the major in charge of security and told him. The major looked alarmed. Within ten minutes my father was told arrangements would be made for them to move to Islamabad later that day. Surely there they could arrange everything?

When my father returned to my mother he said to her, 'You are a great woman. All along I thought Malala and I were the campaigners but you really know how to protest!'

They were moved to Kashmir House in Islamabad, a hostel for members of parliament. Security was still so tight that when my father asked for a barber to give him a shave, a policeman sat with them all the way through so the man wouldn't cut his throat.

At least now they had their phones back and we could speak more easily. Each time Dr Javid called my father the line was usually busy. My father is always on the phone! I rattled off my mother's eleven-digit mobile number and Dr Javid looked astonished. He knew then that my memory was fine.

But my parents still hadn't been told why they couldn't yet fly to me. Later they would discover that the interior minister, Rehman Malik, was hoping to fly with them so they could have a joint press conference at the hospital, and it was taking some time to make the arrangements. He also wanted to make sure they didn't ask for political asylum in Britain, which would be embarrassing for his government.

It ended up being ten days before my parents came but it felt like a hundred days. It was boring and I wasn't sleeping well. I stared at the clock in my room. The changing time reassured me I was alive and I saw for the first time in my life that I was waking early. Every morning I longed for 7 a.m. when the nurses would come. The nurses and Dr Fiona played games with me. The nurses and hospital staff felt sorry for me in a far-off land away from my family. They were very kind, particularly Yma Choudhury, the jolly director of operations, and Julie Tracy, the head nurse, who would sit and hold my hand.

They went clothes shopping to buy me things. They had no idea how conservative I was or what a teenage girl from the Swat Valley would wear. They went to Next and British Home Stores and came back with bags of T-shirts, pyjamas, socks and even bras. Yma asked me if I would like shalwar kamiz and I nodded. 'What's your favourite colour?' she asked. Pink, of course, was my reply.

They were worried I wasn't eating. But I didn't like the hospital food and I was worried it was not halal. The only things I'd eat there were the nutritional milkshakes. 'What do you like?' they asked me. 'Fried chicken,' I replied. Yma discovered there was a halal Kentucky Fried Chicken at Small Heath and would go there every afternoon to buy me chicken and chips. One day she even cooked me a curry.

To keep me occupied they brought me a DVD player. One of the first movies they got me was *Bend It Like Beckham*, thinking the story of a Sikh girl challenging her cultural norms and playing football would appeal to me. I was shocked when the girls took off their shirts to practise in sports bras and I made the nurses switch it off. After that they brought cartoons and Disney movies. I watched all three Shrek movies and *A Shark's Tale*. My left eye was still blurry so I covered it when I watched, and my left ear would bleed so I had to keep putting in cotton-wool balls. One day I asked a nurse, 'What is this lump?' placing her hand on my tummy. My stomach was big and hard and I didn't know why.

'It's the top of your skull,' she replied. I was shocked.

After I started to speak I also walked again for the first time. My first few steps were such hard work it felt as if I'd run a hundred kilometres. The doctors told me I would be fine, I just needed lots of physiotherapy to get my muscles working again.

One day another Fiona came, Fiona Alexander, who told me she was in charge of the hospital press office. I thought this was funny. I couldn't imagine Swat Central Hospital having a press office. Until she came I had no idea of the attention I'd attracted. The hospital started giving daily news briefings on my condition.

People just turned up wanting to see me – government ministers, diplomats, politicians, even an envoy from the Archbishop of Canterbury. Most brought beautiful bouquets. One day Fiona Alexander brought me a bag of cards, toys and pictures from people all over the world wishing me a speedy recovery, many of them schoolchildren. I was astonished and Fiona laughed. 'You haven't seen anything yet.'

She told me there were sacks and sacks more, about 8,000 cards in total, many just addressed, 'Malala, Birmingham Hospital'. One was even addressed, 'The Girl Shot in the Head, Birmingham', yet it had got there.

Rehanna told me that thousands and millions of people and children around the world had supported me and prayed for me. Then I realised that people had saved my life. Most precious of all perhaps was the parcel that came from Benazir Bhutto's children. Inside were two shawls that had belonged to their late mother.

I realised what the Taliban had done was to make my campaign global. Gordon Brown, the UN special envoy for education and former prime minister of Britain, had launched a petition under the slogan 'I am Malala' to demand that no child be denied schooling by 2015. There were messages from heads of state and ministers and movie stars. Beyoncé had written me a card and posted a photo of it on Facebook. Selena Gomez had tweeted about me and Madonna had dedicated a song. There was even a message from my favourite actress and social activist, Angelina Jolie – I couldn't wait to tell Moniba.

I didn't realise then that I wouldn't be going home.

16

'They have snatched her smile'

The day my parents flew to Birmingham I was moved out of intensive care and into room 4, ward 519, which had windows so I could look out and see England for the first time. All I could see were red brick houses and streets.

Dr Javid told me my parents were coming and tilted my bed so that I was sitting up to greet them when they arrived. I was so excited. Then the door opened and there were the familiar voices saying their nicknames for me, '*Jani*' and '*Pisho*'. There they were, kissing my hands as they were frightened to touch me.

I wept loudly. All that time alone in hospital I hadn't cried, even when I had all those injections in my neck or the staples removed from my head. But now I could not stop. My father and mother were also weeping. It was as if all the weight had been lifted from my heart. I felt that everything would be fine now. 'We missed you, Malala', said my brothers, though they were soon more interested in all the teddies and gifts.

I could see my parents were disturbed by how I looked. Before they came in, Dr Javid had warned them, 'The girl you will see is only 10 per cent recovered. There is still 90 per cent to go.' But they had no idea that half my face was not working and that I couldn't smile. My left eye bulged, half my hair was gone and my mouth tilted to one side. I also couldn't hear from one side, and I spoke in baby language as if I was a small child.

My father lamented to my mother, 'The Taliban are very cruel – they have snatched her smile.'

The United Nations announced they were naming 10 November, one month and a day after the shooting, Malala Day. I didn't pay much attention as I was preparing for a big operation the following day to repair my facial nerve. I was taken into theatre on 11 November for a surgeon called Richard Irving to carry out the operation. Repairing the nerve was such delicate work that it took eight and a half hours.

The operation went well, though there was a three-month wait before the left side of my face started working bit by bit. I had to do facial exercises every day in front of my small mirror. To my delight I could soon smile and wink my eye, and week by week my parents saw more movement coming into my face. Afterwards Mr Irving said it was the best outcome he had seen in twenty years of facial nerve surgery, and it was 86 per cent recovered.

The other good result was that finally my headaches lifted and I started reading again. I began with *The Wonderful Wizard of Oz*, one of a pile of books sent to me by Gordon Brown. I loved reading about Dorothy and how, even though she was trying to get back home, she stopped and helped those in need like the cowardly lion and the rusty tin man.

Dorothy had to overcome a lot of obstacles to get where she was going, and I thought if you want to achieve a goal, there will be hurdles in your way but you must continue. Afterwards I told my father all about it. He was very happy because he thought if I could memorise and narrate such detail then my memory must be fine – although I didn't remember anything about the shooting and kept forgetting the names of my friends.

I worked hard in the gym and with the physiotherapist to get my arms and legs working properly again and was rewarded on 6 December with my first trip out of the hospital. Yma arranged for two staff to take me and my mother to the Birmingham Botanical Gardens, not far from the hospital. When we entered the gardens, and I saw all the green plants and trees, it was a powerful reminder of home. It was an ice-cold day so we went into the café and had delicious tea and cakes, something called a 'cream tea'.

Two days after that I had my first visitor from outside the family – the president of Pakistan, Asif Zardari. The hospital did not want him to come as they knew it would mean a media frenzy, but it was difficult for my father to refuse. Not only was Mr Zardari our head of state but he had said the government would pay all my medical bills, which would end up being around £200,000. They had also rented an apartment for my parents in the centre of Birmingham so they could move out of the hostel in the university that they were staying in.

The visit was on Saturday, 8 December, and the whole thing was like something out of a James Bond movie. There were a lot of journalists gathered outside from early on, who assumed the president would be brought to me in the hospital. Instead I was wrapped up in a big purple parka with a hood, taken down through the staff entrance and driven to the hospital offices. We drove right past journalists and photographers and they did not even notice. When Zardari and his party arrived they were brought in through the back.

The president came in to see me with his youngest daughter, Asifa, who is a few years older than me. They brought me a bouquet of flowers. Mr Zardari told the high commissioner to give my father a post as education attaché so he would have a salary to live on and a diplomatic passport so he would not need to seek asylum to stay in the UK. My father was relieved as he was wondering how he would pay for things. Gordon Brown, in his UN role, had also asked him to be his adviser, an unpaid position. The president said that was fine, he could be both.

After the meeting Mr Zardari described me to the media as 'a remarkable girl and a credit to Pakistan'. But still not everyone in Pakistan was so positive. Some people were saying my father had shot me, or that I wasn't shot at all, and we had staged it so we could live overseas.

The new year of 2013 was a happy one when I was discharged from hospital in early January finally to live with my family again. The

Pakistan High Commission had rented two serviced apartments for us in a building in a modern square in the centre of Birmingham. We were so happy to be a family again.

Once a week I Skyped my friends back in Mingora and they told me they were still keeping a seat in class for me. The teacher had brought to class my Pakistan studies exam from that day, the day of the shooting. I had got 75 out of 75.

I was getting stronger every day, but my surgery wasn't over. I still had the top of my skull missing. The doctors were also concerned about my hearing. On Saturday, 2 February, I was back in the Queen Elizabeth Hospital to be operated on by Anwen White. First she removed the skull bone from my tummy, but decided not to put it back as it had not kept well and there was a risk of infection. Instead she did something called a titanium cranioplasty (I now know lots of medical terms!) and fitted a titanium plate in my head with eight screws to do the job of a skull and protect my brain.

While I was in surgery Mr Irving, the surgeon who had repaired my nerve, put a small electronic device called a cochlear implant inside my head near the damaged left eardrum. He told me that in a month they would fit the external part on my head, and then I should be able to hear. I was in theatre for five hours with three operations, but was back in the apartment within five days. A few weeks later when the receiver was fitted behind my ear, my left ear heard *beep beep* for the first time. To start with, everything was like a robot sound, but soon it was getting better and better.

We human beings don't realise how great God is. He has given us an extraordinary brain and a sensitive, loving heart. He has blessed us with two lips to talk and express our feelings, two eyes that see a world of colours and beauty, two feet that walk on the road of life, two hands to work for us, a nose that smells the beauty of fragrance, and two ears to hear the words of love. As I found with my ear, no one knows how much power they have in their each and every organ until they lose one.

I thank Allah for the hard-working doctors, for my recovery, and for sending us to this world where we may struggle for our survival. Some people choose good ways and some choose bad ways. One person's bullet hit me. It swelled my brain, stole my hearing and cut the nerve of the left side of my face in the space of a second. And after that one second there were millions of people praying for my life and talented doctors who gave me my own body back.

People prayed to God to spare me, and I was spared for a reason – to use my life for helping people. When people talk about the way I was shot and what happened, I think it's the story of Malala, 'a girl shot by the Taliban'. I don't feel it's a story about me at all.

Epilogue

One Child, One Teacher, One Book, One Pen . . .

Birmingham, August 2013

In March we moved from the apartment to a rented house on a leafy street. All our belongings are still in Swat, so our house feels big and empty. It sits behind an electric iron gate and it sometimes seems as if we are under a kind of luxury house arrest. At the back there is a large garden with lots of trees and a green lawn for me and my brothers to play cricket on.

If I look out, I see my mother wandering around the garden, her head covered by a shawl, feeding the birds. She is giving the birds the remains of our dinner from the night before and there are tears in her eyes. We eat much the same here as we did back home – rice and meat for lunch and dinner. Breakfast is fried eggs, chapattis and sometimes also honey, a tradition started by my little brother, Atal, though his favourite Birmingham discovery is Nutella sandwiches. But there are always leftovers.

My mother is sad about the waste of food. She is remembering all the children we fed in our house, so they would not go to school on empty stomachs, and wondering how they are faring now. We didn't have much money and my parents knew what it was like to be hungry.

My mother never turned anyone away. Once a poor woman came, hot, hungry and thirsty, to our door. My mother let her in and gave her food and the woman was so happy. 'I touched every door in the *mohalla* and this was the only one open,' she said. 'May God always keep your door open, wherever you are.'

When I came home from school in Mingora I never found my house without people in it. All the women of the neighbourhood used to gather in the afternoons on our back porch. Now I long for guests. I know my mother is lonely. She is always on the phone to everyone back home. It's hard for her here as she does not speak any English. Our house has all these gadgets, but when she arrived they were all mysteries to her and someone had to show us how to use the oven, washing machine and TV.

As usual my father doesn't help in the kitchen.

110

I tease him, '*Aba*, you talk of women's rights, but my mother manages everything! You don't even clear the tea things.'

There are buses and trains but we are unsure about using them. My mother misses going shopping in Cheena Bazaar. She is happier now that a friend with a car can take her shopping.

A door bangs in the house and my mother jumps – she jumps these days at the slightest noise. She often cries and then hugs me. 'Thank God Malala is alive,' she says. Now she treats me as if I was her youngest rather than her eldest child.

I know my father cries too. He knows people say it's his fault that I was shot, that he pushed me to speak up like a tennis dad trying to create a champion, as if I don't have my own mind. It's hard for him. All he worked for – for over twenty years – has been left behind: the school he built up from nothing, which now has three buildings with 1,100 pupils and seventy teachers. He says, 'It's as if you planted a tree and nurtured it – you have the right to sit in its shade.'

His dream in life was to have a very big school in Swat providing quality education, to live peacefully and to have democracy in our country. In Swat he had achieved respect and status in society through his activities and the help he gave people.

My father spends much of his time going to conferences on education. I know it's odd for him that now people want to hear him because of me, not the other way round. I used to be known as his daughter, now he's known as my father. When he went to France to collect an award for me he told the audience, 'In my part of the world most people are known by their sons. I am one of the few lucky fathers known by his daughter.'

A smart new uniform hangs on my bedroom door, bottle-green instead of royal blue. In April I was well enough to start school in Birmingham. It's wonderful going to school and not having to feel scared as I did in Mingora, always looking around me on my way to school, terrified a *talib* would jump out.

It's a good school. Many subjects are the same as at home, but the teachers have PowerPoint and computers rather than chalk and blackboards. We have some different subjects – music, art, computer studies, home economics, where we learn to cook – and we do practicals in science, which is rare in Pakistan. Even though I recently got just 40 per cent in my physics exam, it is still my favourite subject. I love learning about Newton and the basic principles the whole universe obeys.

But like my mother, I am lonely. It takes time to make good friends like I had at home, and the girls at school here treat me differently. People say, 'Oh, that's Malala' – they see me as 'Malala, girls' rights activist'. Back in the Khushal School I was just Malala, the same double-jointed girl they had always known, who loved to tell jokes and drew pictures to explain things.

I describe life in England to Moniba when we Skype. I tell her of the streets with rows of identical houses. I tell her I like England because people follow rules, they respect policemen and everything happens on time. The government is in charge and no one needs to know the name of the army chief. I see women having jobs we couldn't imagine in Swat. They are police and security guards. They run big companies and dress exactly as they like.

I don't often think about the shooting, though every day when I look in the mirror it is a reminder. The nerve operation has done as much as it can. I will never be exactly the same. I can't blink fully and my left eye closes a lot when I speak.

It is still not definitely known who shot me,

but a man named Ataullah Khan said he did it. The police have not managed to find him but they say they are looking.

My world has changed so much. On the shelves of our rented living room are awards from around the world. I've even been nominated for the Nobel Peace Prize, the youngest person ever. I am grateful for the awards, but they only remind me how much work still needs to be done to achieve the goal of education for every boy and girl. I don't want to be thought of as 'the girl who was shot by the Taliban' but 'the girl who fought for education'. This is the cause to which I want to devote my life.

On my sixteenth birthday I was in New York to speak at the United Nations. It was daunting, but I knew what I wanted to say. I wrote the speech for every person around the world who could make a difference. I wanted to reach everyone living in poverty, those children forced to work and those who suffer from terrorism or lack of education. Deep in my heart I hoped to reach every child who could take courage from my words and stand up for his or her rights.

I wore one of Benazir Bhutto's white shawls over my favourite pink shalwar kamiz. I called on the world's leaders to provide free education to every child in the world. 'Let us pick up our books and our pens,' I said. 'They are our most powerful weapons. One child, one teacher, one book and one pen can change the world.' The audience gave me a standing ovation. My mother was in tears and my father said I had become everybody's daughter.

Something else happened that day. My mother allowed herself to be publicly photographed for the first time. As she has lived her life in purdah and never unveiled her face on camera before, it was a great sacrifice and very difficult for her.

Today we all know that education is our basic right. Islam says every girl and every boy should go to school. In the Quran it is written, God wants us to have knowledge. I know it's a big struggle. Around the world there are 57 million children who are not in primary school, 32 million of them girls. Sadly in my own country, Pakistan, 5.1 million children don't even go to primary school. We have almost 50 million adults who can't read or write, two-thirds of whom are women, like my own mother.

Girls continue to be killed and schools blown up. In March there was an attack on a girls' school in Karachi that we had visited. A bomb and a grenade were tossed into the school playground just as a prize-giving ceremony was about to start. The headmaster, Abdur Rasheed, was killed and eight children hurt. In June in the city of Quetta a suicide bomber blew up a bus taking forty pupils to their all-girls' college. Fourteen of them were killed. The wounded were followed to the hospital and some nurses were shot. It's not just the Taliban killing children. Sometimes it's drone attacks, sometimes it's wars, sometimes it's hunger.

Over the last year I've seen many other places, but my valley remains to me the most beautiful place in the world. I don't know when I will see it again but I know that I will. I wonder what happened to the mango seed I planted in our garden at Ramadan. I wonder if anyone is watering it so that one day future generations of daughters and sons can enjoy its fruit.

Today I looked at myself in a mirror and thought for a second. Once I had asked God for one or two extra inches in height, but instead he made me as tall as the sky, so high that I could not measure myself.

I love my God. I thank my Allah. By giving me this height to reach people, he has also given me great responsibilities. Peace in every home, every street, every village, every country

– this is my dream. Education for every boy and every girl in the world. To sit down on a chair and read my books with all my friends at school is my right. To see each and every human being with a smile of happiness is my wish.

I am Malala. My world has changed but I have not.

Malala Yousafzai interviewed by her US editor, Judy Clain

Judy: It's been two years since your book was published all over the world. Would you say that you have a 'regular' life now?

Malala: Now my day is just the normal day of any student. My mother or father has to come into my room to wake me up. I can never get up early on my own! Everyone treats me like a normal girl at school. By now I've made a lot of friends. When I come home from school I like to rest a little bit, because there's always an interview or a programme of some sort. So that's my normal day. And if there's not a lot to do I just spend my time listening to news or music. Other than that I just do my homework.

J: Tell me about your parents. How's your mother doing? What has changed for her? Do you think she's the one for whom things have changed the most?

M: In the beginning and even now it is quite difficult for her to live in this new place which is totally different in cultural tradition. She cannot speak English. Even though she does go to the market, she needs someone to help her get a taxi, to talk to shopkeepers. She does not find a lot of people to relate to. In our country, Pakistan, your neighbours are like your brothers and sisters. They come to your house. You go to their house. In the UK it's quite different. Here, people don't really have that spirit of neighbours meeting each other. It's not the spirit of community.

J: And what about for your brothers?

M: Atal is fine. Atal got used to the UK really quickly. He adapted to this new environment more quickly than us. Khushal is also adapting, but he's taking a little more time. Other than that my brothers are still naughty and enjoy fighting with me! And I also fight with them sometimes. But I always believe that if they are fighting with me I should fight back.

J: What's the most surprising thing for you about living in the West, living away from Pakistan?

M: Well, the thing that I always think about is that – in the UK, although probably not in all the Western countries – people follow traffic rules and they don't honk their horns all the time! It's calm and quiet. It's quite nice and quite surprising that there is a country where everyone follows the traffic codes.

J: That's funny. Is your dream still to return to Pakistan?

M: Yes, I miss Pakistan and I miss my country. It's a beautiful country. I know that people think that there are terrorists in our country and that the situation is really bad, but the fact is that Pakistan is a very beautiful country. We have four seasons, we have mountains, glaciers, forests, hills and deserts. Pakistan is such a beautiful place, and I am hopeful that peace will come and that I will be able to return to Pakistan and continue my work there. I started thinking about education and working with the Malala Fund right at the time when I was shot. I had this dream to see every child educated by looking at people all around me in Pakistan, children who were going to other people's houses to clean their clothes, to wash their dishes. I wanted to see those children with books in their hands, learning and going to school, wearing a uniform – it has always been my dream. And I am hopeful that I will go back to Pakistan and I will finish this dream and that this dream will come true.

About Quick Reads

Quick Reads are brilliant short new books written by bestselling writers. They are perfect for regular readers wanting a fast and satisfying read, but they are also ideal for adults who are discovering reading for pleasure for the first time.

Since Quick Reads was founded in 2006, over 4.5 million copies of more than a hundred titles have been sold or distributed. Quick Reads are available in paperback, in ebook and from your local library.

To find out more about Quick Reads titles, visit
www.readingagency.org.uk/quickreads
Tweet us 🐦 @Quick_Reads #GalaxyQuickReads

Quick Reads is part of The Reading Agency,
a national charity that inspires more people to read more, encourages them to share their enjoyment of reading with others and celebrates the difference that reading makes to all our lives.
www.readingagency.org.uk Tweet us @readingagency

The Reading Agency Ltd • Registered number: 3904882 (England & Wales) Registered charity number: 1085443 (England & Wales) Registered Office: Free Word Centre, 60 Farringdon Road, London, EC1R 3GA The Reading Agency is supported using public funding by Arts Council England.

We would like to thank all our funders:

LOTTERY FUNDED

 **has something for everyone**

Stories to make you laugh

Stories to make you feel good

Stories to take you to another place

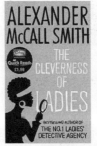

Stories about real life

Stories to take you to another time

Stories to make you turn the pages

For a complete list of titles visit
www.readingagency.org.uk/quickreads

Available in paperback, ebook
and from your local library

Discover the pleasure of reading with Galaxy®

Curled up on the sofa,
Sunday morning in pyjamas,
just before bed,
in the bath or
on the way to work?

Wherever, whenever,
you can escape
with a good book!

So go on...
indulge yourself with
a good read and the
smooth taste of
Galaxy® chocolate.

Proudly supports

Start a new chapter

The Anniversary

Edited by Veronica Henry

From family secrets to unlikely romance, from wartime
tragedy to ghostly messages, *The Anniversary* is a wonderful
collection of short stories from some of the best writers
around to celebrate 10 years of Quick Reads.

This collection includes specially written short fiction from
Fanny Blake, Elizabeth Buchan, Rowan Coleman, Jenny
Colgan, Philippa Gregory, Matt Haig, Veronica Henry,
Andy McNab, Richard Madeley and John O'Farrell.

It also includes delicious anniversary
recipes from The Hairy Bikers.

The Anniversary – something for everyone.

Why not start a reading group?

If you have enjoyed this book, why not share your next Quick Read with friends, colleagues, or neighbours?

The Reading Agency also runs **Reading Groups for Everyone** which helps you discover and share new books. Find a reading group near you, or register a group you already belong to and get free books and offers from publishers at **readinggroups.org**

A reading group is a great way to get the most out of a book and is easy to arrange. All you need is a group of people, a place to meet and a date and time that works for everyone.

Use the first meeting to decide which book to read first and how the group will operate. Conversation doesn't have to stick rigidly to the book. Here are some suggested themes for discussions:

- How important was the plot?
- What messages are in the book?
- Discuss the characters – were they believable and could you relate to them?
- How important was the setting to the story?
- Are the themes timeless?
- Personal reactions – what did you like or not like about the book?

There is a free toolkit with lots of ideas to help you run a Quick Reads reading group at **www.readingagency.org.uk/quickreads**

Share your experiences of your group on Twitter @Quick_Reads #GalaxyQuickReads

Continuing your reading journey

As well as Quick Reads, The Reading Agency runs lots of programmes to help keep you reading.

Reading Ahead invites you to pick six reads and record your reading in a diary in order to get a certificate. If you're thinking about improving your reading or would like to read more, then this is for you. Find out more at **www.readingahead.org.uk**

World Book Night is an annual celebration of reading and books on 23 April, which sees passionate volunteers give out books in their communities to share their love of reading. Find out more at **worldbooknight.org**

Reading together with a child will help them to develop a lifelong love of reading. Our **Chatterbooks** children's reading groups and **Summer Reading Challenge** inspire children to read more and share the books they love. Find out more at **readingagency.org.uk/children**

Find more books for new readers at

- **www.readingahead.org.uk/find-a-read**
- **www.newisland.ie**
- **www.barringtonstoke.co.uk**